T0121544

Where I Belong-

Moments, Mist & Song

Poetry

Smeetha Bhoumik

Editor: Tendai R Mwanaka
Typeset: Tendai R Mwanaka
Cover: **2skywaytripper ©Smeetha Bhoumik**

Mwanaka Media and Publishing Pvt Ltd,
Chitungwiza Zimbabwe

*

Creativity, Wisdom and Beauty

i

Publisher: Tendai R Mwanaka

Mwanaka Media and Publishing Pvt Ltd *(Mmap)*

24 Svosve Road, Zengeza 1

Chitungwiza Zimbabwe

mwanaka@yahoo.com

www.africanbookscollective.com/publishers/mwanaka-media-and-publishing

https://facebook.com/MwanakaMediaAndPublishing/

Distributed in and outside N. America by African Books Collective

orders@africanbookscollective.com

www.africanbookscollective.com

ISBN:978-1-77906-494-3

EAN: 9781779064943

© Smeetha Bhoumik2019

All rights reserved.

No part of this book may be reproduced or transmitted in any form or by any means, mechanical or electronic, including photocopying and recording, or be stored in any information storage or retrieval system, without written permission from the publisher

DISCLAIMER

All views expressed in this publication are those of the author and do not necessarily reflect the views of *Mmap*.

Mwanaka Media and Publishing Editorial Board:

Publisher/ Editor-in-Chief: Tendai Rinos Mwanaka
mwanaka13@gmail.com
East Africa and Swahili Literature: Dr Wanjohi wa Makokha
makokha.justus@ku.ac.ke
East Africa English Literature: Andrew Nyongesa
nyongesa55.andrew@gmail.com
East Africa and Children Literature: Richard Mbuthia
ritchmbuthia@gmail.com
Legal Studies and Zimbabwean Literature: Jabulani Mzinyathi
jabumzi@gmail.com
Economics, Development, Environment and Zimbabwean Literature: Dr
Ushehwedu Kufakurinani **ushehwedu@gmail.com**
History, Politics, International relations and South African Literature:
Antonio Garcia **antoniogarcia81@yahoo.com**
North African and Arabic Literature: Fethi Sassi
sassifathi62@yahoo.fr
Gender and South African Literature: Abigail George
abigailgeorge79@gmail.com
Francophone and South West African Literature: Nsah Mala
nsahmala@gmail.com
West Africa Literature: Macpherson Okpara
chiefmacphersoncritic@gmail.com
Media studies and South African Literature: Mikateko Mbambo
me.mbambo@gmail.com

iii

Acknowledgements

To my parents and teachers, eternal gratitude. To my family and friends, love. Thanks to all the poetry communities that connect us, letting us share dreams. Many of the poems presented here have been written in response to prompts received at the *Global Poetry Writing Month 2017, 2018,* by The Missing Slate (TMS). Thanks to all who have provided us with thought-provoking, insightful prompts. Thanks to Upal Deb for creating a reservoir of world poetry and letting us share in its bounty. Thanks to my publishers and esteemed poet Tendai Rinos Mwanaka, for believing in my work and giving me this wonderful opportunity. **Identity** appeared in *'Writing Language, Culture and Development, Africa Vs Asia Volume 1 Anthology',* 2018; **Icebergs** appeared in *Muse India 2017;* **Swarovsky** appeared in *Muse India 2017;* **Seeing You- Arrival** appeared in *Life & Legends : Cradle of Civilization to Contemporary Indian Poetry;* **Waves of Love** appeared in *Life & Legends : Cradle of Civilization to Contemporary Indian Poetry;* **Paradise** appeared in *'Writing Language, Culture and Development, Africa Vs Asia Volume 1 Anthology',* 2018; **Sound Space** appeared in *Modern Indian Poetry by Sahitya Acdemy, India, forthcoming 2019;* **In an Ancient Land** appeared in *Neesah 2017;* **Precious Breath** appeared in *Unlikely Stories Mark V, Feb 2018;* **Confessions of a Silent Soldier** appeared in *Unlikely Stories Mark V, Feb 2018*

Contents

Introduction...viii

Identity
Sacred Space...2
Where I come from..4
Mother tongue – Earth...6
O Earth...8
Glow...9
A Dehra me..11
Sound Space...12
Sound flows...14
Rispana 16
Origins – Gold in Sepia 18
Bhalobasha (Love)..19
Understanding..22
Origins – When you came away 27
Origin – River Paudya...29
Tiller, Ma 31
Through the mist 33
Ma, you are in me now 34

Belonging
Rhyme shells 36
To verse 38
Dehra morn 39
Dividing / Uniting 41
Radha-verses-Krishna 43
I call you by my name...45
Beautiful edifices, we 46
Heartbreak...48
Interpretations 49

Dew drops on print..50
They came.............................. 51
Betrayal & beyond..52
Paradise
In music of 'deewana hua badal'...............................54
Song for Hazarika.............................. 55
Bird-song: ghazal 57
Melody...58
Messiah Trees...59
Land of paradise...61
Sapphire dreams 62
Beyond the end 65
Dreams...66
Deewana romantic nomad......................................67
Perception
Not just a stone...70
Icebergs...72
Swarovsky..73
Speaking to a tree..75
Chandeliers make good holders.............................77
Oh, Objects..78
Earth in jade...80
Seeing...81
Jewel eyes...82
Seeing You...84
God in words...86
To You..87
Treasure
Stimulus..89
Ground zero..90
Forgive & Treasure...91
Go I know not where...92
Broom Song..95

To verse...97
Equal earth..98
Arcs of love...99
Lost Junction...101
Seeing infinity...103
Three emblems...105

Reality
Calm before the storm...................................106
You Girl..107
Freedom...108
Four layers...110
Sing me a duet..112
Song sung together......................................113
Noir..114
To you, O Tiller..116
Lost..118
Colour..120
Darkening bright..121
In an ancient land......................................122
Do you believe in magic?................................123

Of Dust
Invincible dust...124
Revered dust..125
Dharu-Hera, Dhasal......................................126
Dust in Raptures..128
List of publications....................................130

Introduction

The poems in this collection symbolise my talismans, wayfinders, weather-vanes, illuminators, pathways, dusty routes or shining gems culled from the deep reserves of the mind where magic is churned over centuries, across aeons...

Way way back, when time and space spread their intertwined expansive net-encrusted welcome, was I here - a speck of dust in the universe, a ray of hope in the making? In some form or the other, am sure, yes. This mind, this incredible juggernaut of intuition, understanding, learning, has been around for millenia, being honed to perfection; and who's to say that its present incubator wasn't linked to it in earlier climes?

There are crystals and gems and holy stones gifted by nature, irradiated with breath-taking colours and magical powers to lift the mind and body to higher spheres. Just like them, surely there are invisible, abstract energies of the mind that string words and thoughts together in never-ending hues, vibrant creations called verse that can alter the course of a life, taking it towards vast open oceans of consciousness...

The poems here are my glowing candles or lighted pathways, faltering shadows or looming darkness, that trace a tiny part of my journey towards an unending light...

Poems

Don't be afraid to leave.... that's the only way you can come back...

Because distances, when we are cloistered together, can elongate like cords of coarse hessian and sometimes strangle and maim....maybe even end....all the beauty!

Pools of contemptuous entitlement that at times fill up pores of a relationship easily gained, must be left out to dry in the sun by itself, regaining inlets of sunlit happiness and freedom, absolving guilt and pain...

I belong to rustling leaves, their veins transparent in swaying branches reaching for the heavens; ecstasy, yes ecstasy, because the sky is blue and the oceans inviting me to go with them on unknown journeys, across horizons far far away where the wind blows in new ways.

Prelude

Sacred Space

A lone butterfly perched on a white rose, the morning seemed to shake itself out of its dreamy languor stretching and smiling up at the sun. It was still early. A pink dawn lingered to the east, the sky looking pure and beautiful with flecks of white clouds in motion. Tendrils of a cool breeze wafted in through the open window, ruffling the sheaf of papers on the study table. Raina smiled throwing up the covers and brought her feet down to the ground in an arc.

It was cold to the touch. December in the Himalayas, in a quaint little place away from the hustle and bustle of the city. She smiled quietly to herself, thinking of the day ahead, and the hours floated before her eyes - starting with tea in the garden, the scent of roses and chrysanthemums adding to the taste of her favourite brew, hours of walking and reading among the pine with a rucksack on her back, then returning to put finishing touches to the manuscript.

She wanted to rush out into the morning in her excitement to start the day, but a part of her held back, wanting to linger and relish every moment, slowly savouring its deliciousness. She shook her head in wonder at the choices she had at her disposal now, and then closed her eyes remembering the stark contrast to those in May! 'Oh God, thank you for carving me out of pain, thank you for keeping the light in me safe, thank you for the promise of rain'. She folded her hands in an unconscious gesture, her heart brimming with gratitude.

As she got up, a tiny back chamber of her mind came alive, bringing forth columns of choking black fumes, erasing all that she loved, all she held dear. She tried to push it away, but images of desperate swerving toppling limbs floated in mid air, suspended, and all around

2

there was a deathly stillness, the silence of one's own. One last look up at the sky, imploring, then a mute darkness, a black-out. She struggled, gasping, flaying her hands...

A tap on her shoulder, a soft kind voice in her ear 'Raina, Raina, it's your turn to speak...'
She came to the present with a jolt, looking around at the sea of expectant faces, the people who had gathered at the launch of 'Sacred Space', her debut poetry collection. Taking a deep breath, she said a soft thank you to the memory of her parents, before going up on stage to talk about the birth of her dream.

dreams as abstract
notions electric
to the touch

Identity

Where I come from...who I am....

I am made of earth, trees, ancient
birdsong and the enchanted river
Rispana that flowed past my grandma's
in Dehradoon. It now flows in my veins

because when I came away it wouldn't
be left behind! It flows on gently now
singing those old favourite songs where
the hills danced around and the trees sang,

that is the real me deep within earth and
skin. There are other outer layers that the
world views in parchments, documents, &
mirrors, where reinforced concrete forms

My limbs, my hair is a halo of neon signs I
find it hard to shake off, and the circles on
my wrists are social mores so old that it
will take a lifetime to be free and done;

My home is a precious longing set amidst
nostalgia and the sound of music moving
towards skies of a new day, a new hope,
somewhere very close to where you stay...

On the street if you see a frozen melody
thawing out on sunny leaves and suddenly
ordering tea, you'll know it's me! There'll be
skyscrapers dangling from both arms, but

don't you mind them, they are such pile-ons!

Mother-tongue: Earth

I speak earth;
ever since I could speak
I've spoken earth,

without knowing it!

Maybe since birth,
I've spoken earth,
its raw cadences in

soft tones flowing on in

the river Rispana beside my
grandma's picturesque home
in the Doon valley, I've always

spoken earth: its syllables
of trees, its barmy breeze
lilting white skies making

music, making words not
contained in dictionaries, but
soaring outside, free as birds

defying descriptions, not besieged.

I speak earth.
I spoke earth.
I'll keep speaking earth,

Earth, I speak you, and I love you. Earth, I live you.
Everything else is a corollary.

(Because to speak you is to know you, and to imbibe everything about you;
we come from you, we are connected together...
And that's the most beautiful truth)

O Earth! *(a ghazal)*

I belong to you O earth, every day every hour
I breathe you & give you my heart, forgetting you?

O earth, I can never do that! That impossible
notion is not for me. Those who are forgetting

your blessings in momentary flickers of the
eye to gaze upon the ephemeral, they are forgetting

the churn of oceans in your bosom, the forests that
rise on your crest, the sun that rises not once forgetting

the tiniest little insect within its bracing rays!
How could I ever forget O earth? This forgetting

is not for me, oh no never! With me is always the
fragrance of your wet earth, myriad trails unforgetting

your gentle music, the magic of your healing touch,
Mysterious moments one can never ever lose by forgetting!

Glow *(a Sestina)*

In the deepening shadows, a glow: tinkling dulcet
verses like hilly streams dotting silent rows, mixing
ethereal, outlandish, down-to-earth, all without cess
oh, none at all, save the promise you make, really
only to yourself, to see it as it is, and not let it clot
like congealed blood, unspoken, a dangerous trick!

Fleeting, ethereal, just a glimpse, is it real? Or a trick
of the eyes to lure you into forests, flush with dulcet
tunes you knew so well. You go anyway, lest you clot
on forbidden territories of sloth, so yes you are mixing
fantasy & reality, dreams & shredded fear really,
even as you hum that old favourite tune without cess;

In search of a golden glow half imagined, is there a cess
on it? The forest is all dark and thunder rolls, an old trick
to frighten even the bold, the darkness is a blindfold really,
you walk on, trembling, hanging on by a thought so dulcet
so dear, that maybe you then shed your fear, and are mixing
visions of utopia with whatever is at hand, before it can clot.

Filaments of a golden light, strung on the night, a clot
half visible gnawing at it with all its might, that is the cess
you have to pay, to stay: fight, fight, fight forever, keep mixing
new elements, new lights, new directions, difficult to trick
into submission, difficult to seduce with false dulcet

tunes so apparent in their folly, transparent, yet invisible really!

Golden light, a golden deer? A chimera, a chiaroscuro? Really
is it just a figment of the imagination, no sound basis, a clot
on the landscapes of mind where all sorts of ripples dulcet
and mellifluous flow? Or is it to be gained with a steep cess
paid out with sieved thoughts, distilled deeds, where no trick
holds you back from seeing it, that golden light, you're mixing.

Go forth into the vast and terrible night, where light is mixing
into shadows creating chiaroscuros or chimeras, or really
playing with your imagination, leading you on towards a trick
it loves best, to test you, throwing up phantoms within, a clot
within you, a dark spot you didn't know you had, it's your cess
you pay to enter ephemeral golden strands with voices dulcet.

And when you've battled chimeras and can hear voices dulcet,
know that the streams were with you all along, asking no cess,
It is your darkness in which chimeras hid, now they're but a clot.

A Dehra Me

In the morning mist
years had gone by and threads broken loose,
the smoking earthen chulha (oven) in front:
its smoke - a rising sea of desires in me;
transparent – tendrils of
futures, pasts and present
all bound together and coiled up.
I sat
smoke all around;
smoke in my eyes
smoke on my face;
wisps of pasts and present,

their caress a gift of

conflict & grace.

Had I become time?

misty coiled smoky-eyed,

scattered, billowing vulnerable lines,

of soot & earthy smudges:

 moments lived- living & dying.

It is what the foothills do to you. Entwine within its chimes.

A Sound Space, Home

Sounds are concentric circles of light that expand
upwards through the sky, forming worlds - one's

own, set in the seven heavens, set in musical scores,
set in magical spheres - called home. Sounds have

fragrance too. And home is not really home forever,
it is a paradise you pass briefly through. But sounds,

sounds stay on forever, sounds are really home!
Their fragrance is effervescent, euphoric spilling forth

fruity scent of lokaat, leechi, amrood, pine and a swiftly
flowing river carrying the hills in its embrace, the

trees in its arms! Do you see hazy distant hills in
a trance around a beautiful valley, its white sky turning

pink at dawn? A slow sweep of soft blush that is
visible across decades, carrying the scent of impossible

dreams! The fragrance of innocence, wild flowers, roses,
distinct Dehradoon caresses — *lines of old hindi songs..*

Do you see the love birds playing with the breeze, nary
a care, nor form? (*dil tera, deewana hai sanam... jante*

ho tum, kuchh na ka henge hum...old hindi song).

Sounds are eccentric circles of flour becoming enticing
cake with hilly springtime flecks - vanilla, strawberry,
rose, mountain dew, mother's touch, pecks.

(akele akele... kahan jaa rahe ho...? mujhe saath le lo
juhan ja rahe ho...going alone?take me with you).

Slowly shut....your e y e s ..... silence.... descends....
quiet... a hush....

The valley returns, as if on cue, returning through the
long absence, its fruit laden roads shy as ever, though

the streets have changed. New names, new homes,
the mind does not register the recent, but strolls

back all the way to the beginning, smelling the rice, the
cupboard of spice that only grandmother handled, not

even mother, though she could pick up the porcelain
donkey filled with cardamom, and the jars of achaar,

mango dried and preserved in oil with fragrant saunf,
spices that lasted a lifetime....

What can I tell you of the scented lanes that lined
a childhood, lighting up a whole world of new beginnings...?

At dead-ends, you could always stroll into that dawn,
take the road flowing down to the river and start all over again!

Sound Flows

Static. Electric. Pulsating
meters of thought flow in
outward rings. Glow is a
blue light of metaphors

that refuses to sing. Just
wants to be there, a mute
witness, while

the dancer enters, stepping
lightly. A train of thought
whizzes by, stopping nowhere.
It drizzles.

The steps remind me of an old
custom, a gnarled old tree in
Didur badi (grandmom's), a
ripe plum full of swing, which

reminds me of that old favourite
song – 'sultans of swing'. Memory
matches step with the nimble footed

dancer going from place to place,
over decades and back & forth...

The lullabies mother used to sing,
a valley full of fruit, trees, her songs,
away from a dark city of derelict
mansions left behind one by one, in
summer afternoons on vacation in
dreaded old Kolkata full of favourite
cousins. Then to Bombay, back home.

Pujo. Ma. Anjali. Prasad. New clothes,
shoes. *Dhak.* Yearly ritual looked forward
to, planned ahead, participated, felt
happy in. Really? Felt happy? Yes, with
just a little bit of dread. Normal. The normal
evenly distributed dread of childhood.

Startling forays into youth, its springs,
the trappings appearing slowly, steadily
until the final bloom, one fine spring day,
a rose in a perfect braid falling over the
breast, in Ma's fine filigreed saree of pink
dreams, nestling next to the text of light,
prisms, convex mirrors of unknown focal
length. A+ in entrance tests, university.

The dancer sways away into oblivion
the gloom of inner chambers swallow

her, the light fades, there's much applause,
one returns to this moment, elastic like a
spring, coiled away...
for future views.

*(Pujo - worship. anjali – offerings, prasad -boon Mother- demon slayer.
We stayed in Bombay, spent vacations in Kolkata and longed for Grandmother's
Dehra)*

Rispana

Pebbles, flowers, dreams along that river bank, mountains
soaring behind; was it just the other day I came away

or another lifetime? I can stand there forever
inhaling a sweetness in the air; so what if I came away,

I did not leave it behind! Every breath of mine, each sweet
song: a tendril of its presence, a loved nuance. I came away

carrying its fragrance in atoms of my being, you are there
with me, O friend, as we stand hand in hand. I came away

to find you, to seek a paradise here and now, its essence
infused deep, wherever I go. Did you know I came away

carrying a mist in your name? Soft, gentle, its voice is
here to stay. Were we destined to meet as I came away

on its tide? The river gathers its arms around me and
says yes. Its burgeoning flow I'd seen as I came away

and then a mere shadow of its being, a disappearing
tide, saddened me so. I'll remember her as I came away

full fragrant flowing with all its beauty and might
giving life, giving breath till this day, even as I came away

into new worlds, new dreams. You by my side.

Origins

Gold in Sepia, Baba

An old sepia tinted photograph of yours Baba, has weathered
erasures & survived storms, looking on with kindly eyes through
so many decades of formation, transformation and metamorphosis,
that today your benevolent eyes seem to look straight at me and
not at your professor seated in front, as you defend your thesis.
The blackboard behind you is scribbled top to bottom with equations
and abstract notions I have always found hard to fathom, though I
have tried.   You know that.

Your thermodynamics and entropy havenow become a part of me,
revealing their secrets in a way thatinforms the words I weave! A
manuscript I am working on, speaks of them in odd new ways.You
will be so happy Baba! Though I could not ride into their mystifying
whirlpool with you, they do have a veryspecial understanding in my
heart. The chaos that entropy predictsfor all natural systems, the
astonishing equilibrium attained by waterat its Triple Point, where all
three phases – ice, water, vapour, coexist!What if such precise fact
and notions could translate in a search for peace?

Bhalobasha (Love)

The boat moved gently on the still surface of forlorn waters,
                       eyes catching the gold of the rising sun;

last night's downpour, the blood and mayhem
              hidden forever, an alcove of unopened
              cinnamon

             standing guard on departures, bloodshot,
                  all gone!

An old rusty door, new birdsong,
          years later
               memories come airborne:

rustle of leaves, a silent rush of soliloquy
temple chimes, tinkling bells of cows coming home,

all in ghostly tales of bygones -
             golden shadows of long-ago 'Shirajganj' homes.

In a lighted funnel of dust, a melody rises
easing into this moment its distant sounds
of laughter, of life,
               departures and old songs,

tear drops on the lake's surface

slowly calm down.

They, who left, now reside on the banks of new rivers,
new lives lived away from that golden one
that had bestowed on them all its gold

when they left,

        leaving behind everything,

            but their strength
                their love
                their faith
            in humankind,

        that spring of 1947,
    crossing over an imaginary line....

*They had land and home on the banks of the river Paudya, a huge revered river in
what is now Bangladesh. It was undivided India in my grandfather's time.
Shonar Bangla. Golden Bengal. During the partition in 1947, they came away
from Shirajganj in Pabna jela on the banks of the Paudya.*

*After years of learning and keeping the faith, my father made a whole new life in
a sylvan campus of higher learning, a pioneering professor in a pioneering
institution. A life put together from scratch. With golden memories of golden
'Shirajganj'.*

He was Shona da to all. All his brothers and sisters and even unrelated family shared an uncommon bonhomie, a golden connection throughout life as they had prepared together and reached the helms of their chosen fields.

The gold from the golden land had come with them, embedded within! It took me years to realize that the gold was not in its harvest, its crops, its land, it's skies, but in its men and women....alive in their hearts...and in their minds!

Understanding

The dust rolled up and went skywards in swirling brown scapes, there was an elemental feel to it, as if everything had disintegrated into dust, and I watched in wonder. Early evening, an orange sky aflame with the last rays of a setting sun, the cows returning home in tinkling herds that raised gold-dust with their hoofs. In Bengali it is called 'godhuli logno' the golden hour of home-coming. In the vast open spaces of Dharu-Hera where we were visiting to look at a centuries old ruin of villages long gone, there seemed to be this silent music mixed with gold and dust and ancient song. A scene treasured in my memory, quite unforgettable in its splendour.

Evenings, like mornings, can be quite magical and I remember the ones as a six year old listening to my father as he showed me the stars, constellations, mysterious formations in the sky. I listened all agog as he told me about far away places like Zurich (the sound of the place still holds a fascination for me, enmeshed in memory, beginnings, wonder and a heart full of love); Berlin, Kolkata, Moscow, Paris and of course, Shirajganj (in East Bengal now Bangladesh) where they came from. There was so much love and belonging when he spoke of Shirajganj, I now realise it was a permanent sort of feeling that no departure can take away. When all the family from my father's side got together during vacations or celebrations in Calcutta or Bombay, there was much fond reminiscing about Shirajganj, the place spelt 'love' to my childish ears. The sound of shared joys, memories of a house set in huge acres of fruit and trees, the temple in the home with its revered idols of Radha-Gopinath (the only things that came away with my grandparents when they arrived in India leaving everything behind in 1947), still reverberate in my ears. The difficult times they faced when my freedom-fighting grandfather (an advocate by profession and the President of the district Indian National Congress committee), courted arrest; and they had to live off the land - with its fruits, vegetables, and a predominance of something called 'kochu' a broad leafy vegetable. Deeply etched in my mind forever. Every word. Shirajganj. There's no need for me to visit to relate. There was no need for them to go back to feel the love they had in their hearts for its golden soil, its magnificent river Paudya that had kept them moving and migrating across centuries with its tumultuous presence, its loud heartfelt innocent bonhomie. Long years later, when the tragedy and trauma of Partition slowly loomed up like a slow surfacing iceberg, in history lessons, in books and magazines, I could only wonder at the unsullied hearts and minds of my father's family - they had come away with love and no rancour! The 'gold' of shonar Bangla (golden Bengal), was not in its crops, its fields or sky...it was in the hearts and minds of its people.

Swaraj - my absent minded professor father, loved by one and all for his gentle loving nature and a formidable intelligence that made him a revered presence in engineering academic circles, was extremely generous and went out of his way to be of help to anyone who needed it. And he loved his young students, treating them like friends in an atmosphere where there was a certain distance between faculty and students in the verdant campus I grew up in. I remember the hours they stood in circles chatting away with cigarettes in hand, the circle slowly shifting round and round, and we returned from running in different parts of the campus to find them still talking, still circling.

Moments of happiness. Even as children we understood the strong vibes of connection, overriding our restlessness, our impatience to get him back home.

This adulation of my father, of course, happened in a slow build-up of understanding over years that were marred in the middle by difficulties between my parents. I had sided with mother unconsciously, protecting her from hurt. There was a period of vast distance from my father, an obstinacy in me, that I now wonder at! My brother had preferred to be with him.

And that was because, in his anger father had found it easy to alienate me (words that hurt), even disown, but he did not do that to my brother. I now realize that it is part of the patriarchal thought process that values boys over girls, and he too was a victim of that.

And then to be owned and held close and in adoration...with so much love ! So much love. Ma...

Ma, Mother - a river that flowed in silence carrying love and warmth and bounty. Infinities of belonging, to everything. To song. To music of the universe. Ma.

Ma -brilliant, erudite, warm, soft, gentle Ma. Her father and all her uncles - ICS officers of the British Raj, honest, upright, erudite people. Grandma with her fairy-tale house set in a garden full of fruit trees and fountains and flowers, beside the river Rispana in Dehradoon, my dream valley.

I was born there. In my thoughts I visit there often and stay for long moments, marveling at its miracles.

In reality, everything is long gone. Lost to time and its exigencies. But its song and its music live on forever...in me.

mist and dust fuse together
rising in spirals of
infinite hope

The Universe Series came to life on my canvas
circa 2004,
a magical transformation of my time
and space, through layers of
unifying liberating subconscious
moments
that held so much significance in my life;

and I did not know it then!

I had thought I was inspired only by wondrous images
from NASA, their breathtaking luminous intensity and
beauty that had started me off on this adventure on
canvas with oils as my magic wand!

On hindsight joining the dots and writing about this,
it is clear that the genesis of their mysterious appearance
on canvas of their own volition, bears relation to
what has transpired before, much before, the seeds of their

existence sown in a child's mind, to bear fruit later...

in tilled earth - the mind
seeds of the
universe

Origins

When you came away

Of your fields, home, maps, trees, no sign
only tales of them, in your heart enshrined;

of a river, lost & lonely, calling you to remind
of its currents swift & strong, in your life-lines.

Temple at home, its bells with school's chimed,
you grabbed your slate pencil to be just in time!

Word images are all we have of your golden frieze
innocent days in the wind, river, playing the breeze,

at a standstill when that vast deadly stormy night
so many of you crossed over, taking the stars as light!

Lost land, lost homes, but in your heart a universe soared
taking you across boundaries into new directions & hope,

you cut through the darkness and lighted a lamp
in every heart that you met, your teachings still stand,

tall as lighthouses, in the minds of your students,
your associates, all who loved you, revered your prudence

your steadfast glow in the midst of upheavals

27

your grace, your love in the thick of it all,

Baba, I never knew until I grew up the darkness that was!
You let only love shine on, eluding the gross

mis-understandings, destruction, mindless violence
That shook the earth and tugged at heartstrings.

Even while regaled with Dadu's stories of freedom-fighting,
I could only imagine river Paudya swirl and roar,

as you crossed it each evening to come back home
after playing with your friends on the other bank, and roam

the fields until dusk fell, and you raced to your study table
to keep up expectations *'aunke akshoy aksho'* fable

'A hundred on hundred' in maths, always, that took you
Everywhere, around the world, its power that you

Carried to heights unknown, everywhere you went, you soared...
You soar... you soar....'Hai Khuda' you said often, a Krishna song

Your lips soften, for Radha Gopinath are the only things
You brought with you that evening in '47's divided spring.

River Paudya

The river boomed
far away, your *Paudya* now in our veins
over boulders of time space &
nation, seeking its sense of self.

It smoulders scaling new heights
in search of a renewed identity, negotiating
boundaries, languages, beliefs, rights
longings & hidden quirks known only to
some.

It rages, tumbles, falls, morphs, meanders
and flows to remain the same, overs years
and over terrain, blood to water, water to blood
and back, the *Paudya* now flows in our veins!

We who haven't seen Shirajganj, your beloved land
where the Paudya flowed and where you crossed
it each evening to go play on the opposite bank...

That *Paudya* we carry in our veins now, it was
inevitable, there was nowhere else it could go.
The land, the house you left behind — and also the fruits
& the trees; you brought with you only Gopinath and
Radha from the temple, their love a beautiful frieze!

Paudya came flowing in your arms as you crossed
eloquent taut borders into new land, through lines
and partitions that did not permeate your heart-land.

Your *Paudya* flowed unceasing, restless as you
traversed countries & continents to find your
space under the sun, like a moving beam shining
on its own momentum....
The flowing monikers reflected a kaleidoscopic
multitude of identities augmenting and upholding
each others' longings - freedom, learning, kinship
with golden lands....*amar shonar Bangla....India*

Paudya, you flow on forever in our veins, infusing
a love for an unseen land, getting hazier, farther
and farther & farther... vanishing now as time flows in
other directions, other destinations of its own... but
the love remains.... a deep bond with all.

a kintsugi touch with roses & gold,

may we bring to our wounds of old,

a sparkle of hope our chasms unveil,

planting love where darkness steals...

Ma

Tiller

Of absences really,
of the bent head and absorbed back,
as he tended the waiting earth, that were
conspicuous by their absence when he did not come...

His bent head and absorbed back that were
missing in the beautiful garden, so it is
of absences really.

No defining features, just a hazy memory, scented
with roses, wet earth, dried leaves and smoke from
woodpiles in the backyard, where the lilies were.

Of absences really
because when at work, he became invisible
much like my mother, who we took so much for granted
that she became conspicuous only by her absence.

Her bent-head and absorbed-back as she bent
over the kitchen table cutting vegetables
preparing our meals.

Maya

Wet earth. It always reminds me of childhood, rain, the scent of revival.

Wet earth. It never ceases to make me wonder. Offers me a smile I return.

Wet earth. I care. For you. Precious, fragile, rich, vulnerable, beautiful earth

Wet earth. My prayer. My song. My home.

Wet earth. I love you.

Wet earth. I stop here, or else the rivers, they will flood,

my eyes, her name, my mother…. earth….My Ma was called Maya.

Through the Mist

was not a mist in your name
kept in the vault between tree &
a garden-bench still green, an
old favourite fragrance of jasmine
that went up trellises, linking shells
& dreams, while the trains came in,
soaked in rain...?

the red coolies heaved, pulled
hauled up hold-alls and belongings;
we kept looking back,
as they stood there,
drenched,
then the tonga slowly picked up speed.

Were not traces of memory found
in that lingering lane where all our
journeys had begun together, now
strewn across myriad fine lines
that caress the earth; easing while taking
away togetherness, its supple proximity
to beginnings, to ends, and to everything
held in between...

looking up....sky, oh, you know everything!
what is there to say?

sweet surrender, because rains bring back everything,
memories...dreams....beginnings....

Origins

Ma, you are in me now

I see 'shorshe-eelish', its golden layer of mustard and green chillies
emanating from ardent pressing of mustard seeds to a fine paste on
sheel noda or seel batta (pestle), hands wrung, washed, dried on ends
of sari, now placing golden bowls of rice and fish before hungry
mouths. After all these years, the scene is fresh, like the fish so
carefully selectedby Baba at the market, and meticulously cooked to
perfection by Ma. Home.

Ma, Masters in literature and philosophy. Ma, with a deep love for
poetry, Ma,the lonely little girl addicted to books, pen-friend to
Shibram Chakroborty, Ma, married off terminating further studies,
or ambition, because Baba was toogood to miss !

Ma. shorshe eelish, pabda jhol, tomator chutney, bhaja mugger dal,
alu bhaja,phulkopir torkari. Ma, abol tabol, Rabindranath Tagore,
Sukumar Ray, PatherPanchali. Ma, ' *rannaghore dhukte hobena, homework
shesh koro.*'('Don't enterthe kitchen, finish your homework'). Fluent in
three languages Bangla, Englishand Hindi, unlike Baba who knew
only two. Ma, brought up in Shimla, herDad, an officer of the Raj,
huge bungalows, beautiful gardens, khanshamas

who whisked up delicacies at a moment's notice, and Ma in the
library, pouringover books.

Ma, the one we knew, pouring over the kitchen table at all hours,
yellow stainson sari, a fresh marinade of fish just out, maybe cutlet,
maybe fries, maybe jhol.
That's all we could think of then. We did not know she had topped
university and had received very special recommendations for a
doctorate. Years later,meeting Mrs Dhanmasi at Indraprasth college,
we were so surprised! It wasalmost impossible to imagine. Baba was
our hero, our model, the much lovedengineering Professor of
international repute. Ma just a shadow offering solace
and food.

Ma, you must know I don't love to cook, but have so many recipes
by heart,
Oh, I have a special nook for recipe books!

Belonging.

Rhyme Shells

Its finer crust is visible from far, not just
the shell but its inner light too, the warm
golden welcome and the friends, all hearts
pouring words into cups, in goblets, in vines
of miraculous verse, floating in its air, its
very atmosphere, and I long to be there
soon,
      within its flowing words, such

      A magical universe!

You'll see a wave of golden
haze,
      shimmer of dust,

      A lilting grace,

     streaming forth mellifluous
      Odes to existence;

and berating all that robs it,
reduces it, wrinkles its embrace. It is the
mysterious alchemic abstract world of poems
and verse, all that is precious & loved: its trust

that belongs to this century & the next,
& the previous ones and all of history :
 precious, treasured, loved, set free.

The multi-coloured shells you'll see
are of varied & beautiful patterns, some large
some tiny, with a magical degree, embodying
music of the hills, the forests, the rivers & trees;
you & me, and me & you, all through history!

Not that all is light, or was light, forever and
faraway. The shells speak of such darkness from
their sojourns in tunnels spewing blind engulfing
hate, back then, and right now, that all of the
lucidity of eyes and fluidity of hearts is called
upon,
        to preside over
                returning a light
                    that lies buried within....
                            flesh...and thought... and

                        shells.... in beings.

Verse, to You

A song draped in mist & memory sways this golden spring day,
It carries the scent of pine, hills in every line, to this very day;

If you feel a speck of dust rise and ripple in your hair to play,
It is magic floating in the air, across the years each beautiful day;

Roses, tourmaline, deep sea aquamarine, dreams and paradise
rise & sway, a rare translucence so tranquil this beautiful day,

Lives you touch are sprinkled with gold-dust in mysterious ways,
O Verse, blessed is your touch, every moment, every single day!

In a lighted funnel of dust, a melody rises, slowly, decides to stay,
It is scented with wood-smoke, memory and mist this beautiful day.

A Dehra Morn

The tall stately trees by the gate stood erect, their leaves unruffled by the breeze. The air was fragrant. I looked out across the white boulders to where the Rispana flowed in gentle waves, sparkling silver. The smell of flowers and fruits in my grandmother's garden wafted to me in sudden gusts and I was conscious of a deep feeling of happiness.

Time must have enveloped me in a strange transparent mist through which everything was still crystal clear, across decades and terrains. That moment has become a part of me without my realising it, seeping into every cell and pore of my being, and into my mind and thoughts.

Their thoughts arrive on tip-toe, softly; or at times, the thoughts cascade with the speed of an avalanche!

Just when needed, when the hour hand cries out in despair, and the minutes seem mute with foreboding, thoughts of that fragrant white morning cascade in with the speed of an avalanche, or tiptoe in on soft padded feet, their beauty still crystal clear, divine.

The world gets mired in a tortuous quicksand of dark deeds, with accolades reserved for those who adhere, indeed affirm its cruel needs.

On dusty parallel paths however, thoughts cascade with the speed of an avalanche, assembling an ethereal protective shroud around everything, reaching that pristine pure moment fragrant with life, as if in blessing!

tall oaks so close glowing green

her snow-white hair

a halo around everything

Dividing Lines

Unknown Addresses, Unseen, circa '47

Houses that had lived through turbulence
just like people, carry lines on their faces
sometimes more brooding and deeply etched
than seen on old men from the mountains;
craggy, deep groves of unbreached divides,
ruins of emotions and lives that had not been
spared.

A child's cot, an old photoframe, blood, bone,
penury and shame, posing alongside a broken
kitchen sink, over which algae and fungi had
lovingly draped their caresses, over long dark
winters fraught with fears of so many names
that haunted.

Address Known, Seen

Ink Portrait Two - 13 A, circa '75

A *thakur-ghar* in a mezzanine nook between
the first and ground floors, beat as the heart
Of this *opar bangla* joint family spread over
Four-storied rambling rare bonhomie & warmth,
since their arrival in Kolkata from Shirajganj
1946: a tale of love and winning over odds...

13A Brindaban Mallick 1stLane, opposite
Ram Mohan Library, next to Nandalal sweets
The haunt of childhood summer vacations,
Family weddings, get-togethers in death and
well-being,
Abode of memories.

(Thakur-ghar means God's room in Bengali, 'opar-Bangla' refers East Bengal,
now Bangladesh, across the river)

Belonging

Radha-verses-Krishna

Sweet nothings, or mysterious shells
whispering in your ear, a palm cupped
conch? Or shell-like, a crescent embrace,
drawing you closer, but the wind rustles
scattering the words, and you look around;
an eternity fades...
Even the flowers sound
    impatient in their eloquent grace!

The evening sways as I murmur:
'When do you ever listen to me, pray?'

Gathering your green-blue feathers now,
invisible, you say it is time to leave! The
palm unfolds, swaying to the ground, mute
in gold - an autumnal reed,
eyes droop,
a lone tear from nowhere wets the sky and
spreads to the earth,
    lips quiver,
as i try to utter the evening's last few words,
I long to speak...

Your departing shadow touches those of the

Leaves & branches of the flaming gulmohar
and walks all over me as i silently weep.

(To the beloved 'poetry' with whom it is hide & seek-
A togetherness full of silent distances; and to Radha-Gopinath,
our family deities, the only things my grandfather carried in his
arms when he came over to India)

.

'I call you by my name'

In an ethereal spring aeons ago
   a rose whispered to a mermaid:
     'I call you my name, O fragrance,
       O rose. Amen'. Aquamarine, her
        ice petals shining, resplendent,
          she had written 'mermaid' on
          the blooms that filled her

                    world

         her senses; a glimmer of
       pink & green, delicate, a dream
     awash in lush green canopies of
    sapphire. There were castles in the
   air, knights in shining armour, ships that
 sailed to foreign shores laden with gold, fur,
memories and notions that set the heart afire!

   I call you by my name

 ' *tujhe suraj main kahta tha, magar usme bhi aag hai,*
  tujhe chanda main kahta tha, magar usme bhi daag hai',

    ..... I call you by my name.....
               ...... I call you by my name.....
.... I call you by my name.....

(lines of an old Hindi film song embedded here, with love. 'Tujhe suraj main kahta tha, magar usme bhi aag hai, tujhe chanda main kahta tha, magar usme bhi daag hai' I'd have called you the sun, but it has fire, I'd have called you the moon, but it has spots).

Beautiful Edifices, We

A leaf, its veins ajar
a trove of filigreed moments
through which
we peep, to see ourselves
standing
in the present moment;

Swathed in light
burnt to cinders
of togetherness,
over the years
that have given and taken away
all that we have.
Ants and emotions
walking out, and returning on tiptoe
when it rained!

Iridescent, invisible.

There were diamonds too
on the walls, with mildew,
hewn out of shadow & glimmering
soft tremors of joy
on an uneven glaze of molten
pain,
never again,
we'd promised.

In vain.

Streams of thoughts
play out themselves
in cinematic vision
as the faces rotate.
time is circular here,
not linear with a past
and a future.

This is then
this is now.

Pearls
in the eyes,
a heartful of
diamonds
and a strange
solitude

oh, roses too !

Belonging

Heart-Break

Fragments of moonlight, haibun and coffee linger
long after the night is done and gone in a flurry
of vanishing stars;

salt on the cheeks, unseeing eyes that spied your departing
silhouette: you had brushed past the scented frangipani, &
the flaming gulmohar; oblivious...

The morning breaks out in a silent onslaught of emotion
a cold wind across unmapped terrain, turmoil raging
strong,

shards of light speckle & enter gun-metal eyes - yours, I can
see them now. Cold. Cold. Shorn of care. A silent rage in them
wondering how I could think.... on my own.....and not give in!

Even in heart-break there's a sunrise somewhere on a distant
horizon, I can feel it, more than i see it, I can hear it too, a wild cry
and I cry out in pain, in wonder, and in a loss filled with gain.

Interpretations

Counterintuitive optic-tunnels
                  in steam the hiss of ice
        twin twigs in folios
                                      Far   a   p   a   r t...

    & alter-ego
there is snow melting, the heave of shores,
darkness hidden and
within day's embrace
a naked night

   its presence within :

that hears 'I don't care'
the words ' you'll be fine' floating on thin air
missing fishplates, a certain derailment...

   The interpreter, silent, stoic, expressionless.
shell-shocked, numbed, terrified.

'Dew Drops on Print'

'Dew on the digital print', is not really dew, you know that,
I stand holding the 5 by 8 as you walk away, the whistle
goes one final time, the train starts moving, I move to my
seat. You are receding, now just a movement among the
throngs milling around, the station seems static, frozen
with frenzied movement, hands waving, people moving
trying to keep up with the train, you are receding, you
don't wave and neither do I. I keep looking back, craning

my neck, aware that others are entering the compartment
expecting me to move so they can place luggage under
the bunk, but I keep looking back, though I don't wave &
neither do you, you are still standing there, now just a dot,
the dew gathers as the train picks up speed, spilling over
the digital print, I keep wondering why you gave it to me,
why this last time, when reading between the lines I gather
that we are like the colour left behind after blood has drained...

They Came

They came, singing in the rain
the larks,
their snow-tipped icy shells
about to shatter into smithereens
in force ten winds
blowing north to north-west,
meeting me at the junction;

I stood,
a shadow against the gale,
prepared to play host –
how strange that love & hate
intersect at these junctions.
masks down, baring all
for eternity to see;

The boiling rage of hate
the freezing point of love
knotted here in degrees of restricted freedom
unable to coalesce
unable to cease.
The winds are strong, biting, frosty,
I stand huddled,
as the larks circle up there
their shells falling like meteors all around…
the sound of singing in my ears,

far away, a pink pierces & streaks across the blackness

just a little more...

They came singing in the rain,
the larks.

Betrayal & Beyond

Its dead leaves lie strewn
all around,

    its pervasive touch
        profound,

           in waves of the ocean,

                & on the ground.

        Its touch turns
        all to rust,

    an off-colour, off-kilter
shade
  of grey
    drowned

      in distrust,
       & finely ground

feelings

that hurt to dust
to dust

to death
and beyond.

At last, a liberation
in infinite skies,
an acceptance :

this too shall pass
and in passing
leave a lesson
in its ochre sighs...

Stay equal, stay unmoved
at all times,
what of betrayal,
what of love?
two sides
of the same coin!

Paradise **– in Music**

Inspired by Dreamy Song *'Deewana Hua Badal'*

Fragrant soaring billowing white skies
bloom with enchanted clouds that
dance & float away,

You sway after them, half dreaming.... there's
so much to feel and hear and see - songs
that take you right up to

Paradise and infinity, you dangling somewhere
in between! A song now, you yourself, now a cloud,
now a rainbow, a tree;

melodies that last a lifetime, an eternity, a moment
a dream; you wake in the flowering of gulmohar, a
pink rose in your hair

that wants to dance with the spring,
play in the sunshine, wilt in the afternoon's
drowsy dormant overpowering whim...

Paradise **Your Songs**

The hill and the song, you've moulded as one
a thousand lighted lamps glowing warm,

Hazarika   a feeling that flows through hearts
& rivers washing over boundaries, making

The earth once again one; over aeons and
endless storm, into melody's home! Same &

at once so disarmingly different, innocent
& forlorn, the world that revolves around me

and you and almost every norm. Questions
surface on the roar of rivers, startle into

submission a new dawn... 'why do you flow
on, O Ganga? Why do you keep flowing, in the

face of such unfairness, inequality, injustice?
Why do you?'

O Hazarika, thousands of us keep asking this
with you, after you, with you,

Our hearts ringing, minds open to possibilities,

Bhupen - ways of meandering nomadic justice

Dot the world.
Hazarika. In thousands...
(Humble tribute to Bhupen Hazarika)

Paradise
& bird song:

birds of paradise
carrying all colours :
tolerance soars the sky.

If you'd told me a while ago there's no paradise,
yes, I may have said, but today, oh, today how can I ?

Today, washed within its glow of sonnets, its scent
a river of words in verse, how can I, oh how can I?

Tell me you'll flow on forever thus, joining old wounds,
a kintsugi touch and better than before, so today, how can I?

The birds flying all over the sky, freedom in their wings,
they got me here, and they got you here, so today, how can I?

When you invited me in, you gifted me bits of the sky,
some sonnets and birds too, so today, how can I?

No, today I shall hold back my nod, and only smile with
the day's unfolding, because today, how can I, oh, how can I?

I see you floating some thoughts away like shikaras, the
water rippling in their wake, so today, how can I?

Today, just let me revel in your grace, and make it last forever...

Melody

In a lighted funnel of dust, a melody rises,
    delicate, gossamer,
        strange: a flute in her hands,
            imaginary, out of thin air:

            Old friends for years!

          Grief,
            desolation
              heartbreak
                overwritten in mere moments,

      Infinite possibilities seem all hers!

She's lost in thought, unseeing; her gaze on turquoise green
thoughts that dare, that dream,

and disappear in a lighted funnel of dust; a melody rises,
filling her heart, her mind, her entire being.

Melodies are magical,
so mysterious,

like light
& blessings!

Paradise

Messiah Trees (*a sestina*)

Dew nestling in every leaf, unceasing morn to eve, your breath
a tender 'raga' of melodies we breathe! In your growing shadows
are havens lush green - a shelter for wanderers, toilers, all beings,
& lost souls in search of inner themes. Their songs, their stories
in your translucent veins, in your bark, your leaves a silent work,
so accepting: your gifts. The sky speaks of you as a messiah

a saint, a silent symbol of love, endearment & grace! O Messiah,
to me you whisper secrets of life; with each enchanting breath
it's clear you are shining a new light with your selfless work!
Oh that we took heed and shone on too, leaving behind shadows
of our deeds untrue! Let your melodies play in our hearts, our stories
renewed with kinder thoughts that have a place for all beings.

Miracles do happen, and you are one, yours a warmth for all beings:
in your eyes all equal born, every branch of yours a messiah's
song, raised or lowered in blessings, in dark glades of joyous stories.
We breathe in, breathe out, and mingle with your life-giving breath,
extracting ourselves from inglorious ways, coming out of shadows
into the lambent beauty of a day well spent, a day of kindred work.

Such is your light and the beauty of your being, you touch all work
arduous, tedious, onerous and harrowing, with ease for all beings.
In your deepening glow melts all darkness, bidding adieu to shadows
that threaten in unsavoury ways or digress; and much like a messiah's

touch, you heal with a sudden cool gush, a waft of inhaled breath,
a joyous tiding carried from afar, as in fairy-tales or stories

loved forever, like Geisha & the golden bear, Puss-in-Boots stories
that have come away with us and now are part of our life, our work,
so dear! Do you hear the sound of silence O Tree, that in your breath
becomes a quivering new language of love, spoken by all beings?
Do you hear the drums Tree-O, is it freedom you seek like messiah's
of yore, who with a single touch could banish far away shadows?

In the darkness your leaves glow, a million stars against shadows
that want to devour, a soft knowing awakens the sleeping stories
within ourselves, ones that remind of tireless trails, of messiah-
like zeal to move towards a beautiful, equal world where all work
is pure! It is time now, O Tree, O Messiah, O Being of all beings,
it is time to dismantle demonic rules with ones that ensure breath,

for every man, woman, child, whatever colour their shadows
unfold, just like you uphold in your being, and in your silent work
the countless years of patient messiah-like bearing, your mark!

Land of Paradise

Knock knock knocking on friend's doors, with a few gem-like icebergs & snow, forof earth and her mysteries, there's a story hidden in ice-hills, so precious to atropical woman, with dreams of snow her heart aflame! Have you ever wonderedhow those frozen hills, made of fresh-water and not salty-chills, came to be right there in the middle of the ocean? Icebergs - yes, those icy hidden hills that can onlypartially be seen, much to a ship captain & crew's chagrin. Ah, so hear me now,there is a *Land of Paradise*, deep in the earth's crevice, where, flow currents warm & nice,that are really hidden rivers in tow, flowing right up to the frozen arctic toe; and

gurgling, rolling, euphoric from the *Land of Paradise*, when they burst forth into thefrozen Arctic outside, freezing fingers touch them, kiss them, want to be more thanfriends; but they? Oh, no, they would have none of it, and up in holy smoke they go, scandalized to their warm little core! Standing lofty, tall and spiky, they shoot right up and away from exploring invading eyes, that embarrassed and abashed, retire inawe of their frozen majesty! There, now that their secret is out, you might as well dwellon how, when they overturn, there's a gem-like glow burning in them? Do you think they absorb red rays of anger and emit cool blues, in complete contradiction of their views?

Sapphire Dreams *(a sestina)*

This isn't a poem about departure, it speaks of a lingering presence; a
steady rhythm
that plays on, like streams of hoisted prayer flags in a storm, as the
blues
set the tone of their farewell song. It is to be sung in sapphire, gold,
thirst & trees,
of course, trees, it is for them, it is their song! Deep, a thirst, dark a
heart that flows
on, smoke in the eyes, smoke all around, it was all we could do to
make ourselves dream
of a morrow when they will return. Now it is foggy, shadowy fires
glowing sapphire

in the dying day merging into night, it is not a poem of departure, it is
aglow with sapphire
burning bright in hearts as we remember trees, swaying gently in the
breeze, a rhythm
they've instilled in our lives. Every breath we take, every song we
sing, real or in a dream
we yearn for their return, from worlds where they've gone, leaving us
with the blues,
an ashen loneliness within. How to breathe? How to sing? Inhale
what, exhale, think ? Flows
a gossamer ethereal thought so out of reach and difficult to perceive,
we cut down our trees!

Axe in hand, minds in haze, haphazard, cutting, slaughtering days
that put an end to trees,
for smouldering empires, so out of place in the grand scheme of
things! If only sapphire
lent its truth for a brief instant so the axe shatters and greed
disappears, and love flows
glowing in the bark of sal, sheesham, teak, oak, peepal, amrud, pine
and neem, their rhythm
in our hearts throbbing. The thirst for a song, the need for a tree to
light up rhythms & the blues
within, as vast as the flowing white skies and the night's starry hours
when we dream.

In mellow music, in purple startling dawn, a slow awakening, a wake-
up call, not a dream,
It is real, visceral, flowing in every vein and song - how will we live
once they're gone? Trees
trees, the heart yearns, the breath desires, without them there are no
survivors; the blues
set the evening afire! Face to face with a plastic tree, a tree in a sylvan
sculpture sapphire;
Oh, how ridiculous! How did it come to this? Will there be museums
full of trees, their rhythm
captured in artificial breeze escaping hollows ? An apocalypse even
now flows

as we speak. Listen, this isn't a poem. This is a paean to peace. An
ode to trees. It flows
unbidden, towards reason, it is a golden frieze for all season, it tells us
of our dream

of an equal green earth seeped in love, it is music. It's cadence and
beat and rhythm
reside deep in us, it forms our being, it keeps us going, it lets us
breathe, the music of trees
from the beginning of time to this evening of peace. The music is all
around in rings of sapphire
encircling, endearing, giving us fire, so we may live and breathe. It is a
song of the blues

sung in happiness, holding hands, looking at the future through rose-
tinted eyes, the blues
in the rustle of leaves of spring, the long lonely hours of finding
oneself, it flows
through our days like hilly streams. Now you see them in the
distance, glowing sapphire
so close, yet they're really so far, if only the hours let us be perfect
beings, like in dreams,
all love and quartered desires that crave nothing, save a perfect sky,
and loving trees
Oh, that we were perfect beings! That we sang together, in perfect
harmonic rhythm!

This isn't a poem on departures, it is a song of rhythm and blues,
of bringing back our real treasures, of glimmering miracles - our
trees,
O bring back the trees everywhere, in cities, towns & streets, not just
in dreams.

Paradise?

Beyond the End

Blue lamp on a night train,
rhythmic sway, left to right
right to left, eyes sapphire,
drooping lids loosen their
hold on reality & let the world
go....slowly away, so slowly....

A train speeds on its
way to eternity
into a frozen land!

New architecture of cities full
of light, space & abundance,
no dirth, no furore over rights,
over Gods, or boundaries and
unbounded desires- fights.

Everything is aplenty here,
a purple light glows all the
while, stars twinkle like roses,
and chrysanthemums ...

One can wait here forever for
everyone to arrive, and meanwhile
old old songs play along the

sidewalks; coffee shops send
out heavenly aromas into crystals
of other atmosphere.....

A day in paradise.

Dreams

Hope the heat, the thirst,
sound of empty plates
in this land, melts away
into cascading waterfalls:
of citizens who shape and
mould a better world...

Deewana, O Deewana, *where has the song gone?*

Deewana, oh romantic nomad, madly singing
you turn cartwheels in the air, look how you've
turned the clouds crazy too! Here they come
floating on thin air with nothing but their hearts

on their sleeves! Oh, how will I ever tell them of
beloved Kashmir's eves? How will I tell them of the red
rivers that flow, holidayers, who without love
come and go, their hearts empty of Kashmir's

own folks? Deewana, tell me where all the love
has gone...is it only smoke of gunfire now filling
the valleys shorn of heartbeats, that had all
danced to kahwah lit nights before...? Deewana?

The clouds wait up there after long, looking for
a paradise like before, the streets lined with love
and apple cheeked people carrying fruit baskets
two by four. Now all they'll see is lines of dreaded

camouflage, winding, grinding, smashing through
the red-tinged roofs, the fields strewn with dead
flowers that had names of little girls they'd know.
How will they ever get over this, Deewana?

Will you also, like the others, simply hand me the
usual answers, deny everything, deny knowledge
deny .... Deny.... deny.....de. ny.....de..... ny....
everything....Deewana....?

Lakhon hain yahan dilwale, par pyaar nahin milta,
Ankhon mein kisi ke wafa ka, ikrar nahin milta...

In the misty boulevards peppered with storm,
its gunshots in rainy blood-streams running
parallel to homes, it is a silent anguish, dry-
throated, unheard; over years it has become
the norm!

Outside :
silent storm,
raging within
too.
We keep silent
though
in our decorous homes,
away from it all,
only on vacations,
to return.

Mehfil mehfil ja dekha,
Dil ko kaheeeen, chain na mila,
Main too yaaron Akela hi raha....

Lakhon hain yahan dilwale, par pyaar nahin milta,
Ankhon mein kisi ke wafa ka, ikrar nahin milta...

Lakhs are there with hearts, yet no love abides
In the eyes of none does a care reside

Mehfil mehfil ja dekha,
Dil ko kaheeeen, chain na mila,
Main too yaaron Akela hi raha....

Moving from gathering to gathering
the heart found no solace
I remained alone my friends…

Perception - Not Just a Stone

Its surface striations, earth-marks, rivulets & tiny craters
speak of a million nights out in the open, talking to the
elements - an old eternal conversation between earth, sky,
wind, sea and storm...... It is a small uneven stone we had

Picked up on our trip to the Himalayas, first stop Hardwar-
Rishikesh, where it lay on the river bank, full of beautiful
white boulders and stones. It was small, uneven, standing
sturdy on a strong base, tapering up to a top that made it

Look like a tiny replica of the hills beyond, and a sudden
Love, quite undefined, must have swelled up in his heart,
For my husband picked it up, gazed at it and gruffly handed
it to me. I solemnly bagged it and brought it home, with love.

(old song looms up 'dekh kasam se kasam se, kahte hain
tumse haan...tumbhi chaloge, hath maloge, roothke humse
haan! kya lagai tumne, ye kasam kasam se....?'

Conversations that had stopped....resumed...lyrical)

It rests quietly now in a cosy nest at the head of the bed,
Adjacent to a laughing Buddha, a revolving photo stand of
His triumphant participation in the Mumbai half marathon, my
Husband's timing perfect, and blessed by earthen idols of

Ganesh-Lakshmi above. I am wondering now what it makes
Of this confinement, this restricted existence within four walls
After all those years of open porous osmotic interchange
With the whole of nature and all that breathes within it.

It must have seen a million moons change shape, a thousand
Suns rise and fade away, rise and fade away, and sudden
Storms gather and disappear......the river flowing by in full spate,
Does it miss its swift flow now?

It has gathered in its pores footsteps, whispers, birdsong, rain,
dust smoke, haze and the vibrations of centuries of birth and
death..... birth and death.... In its small uneven frame, there is
More than any man-made article ever enfolds, it is unchanged

Unchallenged, I suddenly see now that it is indestructible!
Of all the things in the house now, this little stone will be the
Only thing that remains.... ever after....everything else will perish…

Icebergs

Little icebergs from Antarctica
had floated down into my native
land, singing with the birds, odd
new songs of enchantment, that
spoke of freedom.

Freedom that melted into dusk, lit
up minds and waves of liberation
came surging in swathes of turquoise
blue, washed with sea green. Sitting
on a rock, we watched mesmerised,
soaking it all in.

Little icebergs that had broken through
all barriers to reach us, shone like lights
on deep dark patterns of ancient mores
held captive for so long, held so close to
the core of an ancient land...

Examined. Illumined. Scrutinised,

The salt in its spray stung old wounds
that wanted to dig in deeper, fester, eat
away inner sanctums. But not anymore,
not now that the icebergs had arrived,

crystal clear in their reflections of the way
we were, the way we must be, and the
way forward....

We all needed to change!

Swarovsky

Delicate eggshell China, Swarovski,
tinkling high heels on the sidewalk,

an elegant entrance, cool confines
fluttering momentarily in the heated

gust that had swept in, unabashed
brazen. Fingers sweeping across in

disdain, a rapid exit, kerchief held
close at hand to ward off the cruel

heat wanting to devour, to disown
those fleeing their own, their kin, in

unashamed upward swings. But it
only succeeded in killing those poor

kin!

Footsteps on the burning asphalt
running naked, arms outstretched,

will it halt her feigned progress? Or
will the wheels roll on, clattering,

clamouring, clawing out eyes, nails
teeth, of those on the street, their

home?

Speaking to a tree

The enchanted:

Roaring revolving worlds
came in with the tide, it
is their sound you hold in
your heart, their shapes
shift. Shadows of a
hungry yesterday are still
here, looking for morsels of
tomorrow; will you give in?

Tree:

In silence, soft murmurs:

Bits of earth change form,
appearing in all sorts of new
avatars, but i see the sky,
the stars, just the same.
The writing on my bark is old
& weathered, the song in my
branches is ever new, eternal,
the birds keep coming.

Like the earth, i'll come to
you in many forms, always-

transforming. You don't
worry for me. As long as
I live, i'll love you.
Stay blessed.

Earth:

Into her dry thirsty skin
a wet drop fell in silence,
it wasn't rain...

Chandeliers make good holders

Of found objects, I'd yet make
a mountain, a river, a forest,

Pieces first strung together
with straw, some sticky rice

Hope and glue. When the sun
shines, and the incandescence

of lost worlds pierces the heart
a chandelier would materialise

and hold up everything: fast,
fervent, furious and true.

Chandeliers make good holders...

Oh, Objects!

Surprised at the close scrutiny, they mocked me
I looked even deeper into them, and they mocked me more!

The earthen pot in which roses had wilted in the summer heat
is a porous, giving kind of thing, though it seemed to mock me too;

I looked at the glass showcase full of curios & mementos, a museum
of travel memories and anniversaries, and it gave me a surprised look.

Taken aback, into the kitchen I went looking for tea, the kettle is an
old repository, a blackness that shades its innocence, its camaraderie,

the teapot, a favourite of mine, seemed to understand and nodded
away to the kettle's effervescent chant, flush with flavour, deft hands.

Out into the morning when I went, the first thing I saw were the
trees,
the trees, their transparent sways in gold and green, a breeze playing

some old theme, trees that held on to the earth in miraculous sweeps
of cemented toe-rings! A cat said meow in passing, opening &
shutting

its eyes, rather odd, I thought, but of course I know all about cats,
my home is their hotspot! They had stretched and washed and were

ready for breakfast when I came in, and the orange plates spread with
whiskas soon needed more helpings. As I looked deeply into his eyes,

a surprised Tom, grooming post breakfast, shot me a baleful look,
not amused, not responding to such funny intrusive acts! I
transferred

my attention now to the potted plant, a beautiful bougainville of pink
and white, and the sweet gentle being seemed to grow an inch right

there, soaking up all the loving curious kindly attention, with rays of
a rising sun.

Morning shows the day, and it opened up shapes of things that
hid abstract notions in them:

                    the innocence embedded in old albums,
their black and white stories now so quaint,

          the power of a melody
to take you back down memory lane,

      some objects have more past in them,
                          some, like the clock, more future,
            a jug of water stands still in the present
                  the fm radio takes me back & forth
                        through time. Am still looking.....

Earth in Jade

Starbursts of fused dreams alight
each night like summer showers on waiting
expectant leaves, seep into minds
and turn the earth a blooming jade green,
or burgundy red, a flaming ochre sheen
and the city in the night wants to enchant thus too!
It brings out its neons, its amethyst
its treasure trove of faux beajoux,
a chest full of promises, only some that are true;
as streams of glittering diamonds, rubies, pearls
sashay through the city in the night, singing blues,
jazz, and all that razzmatazz
the dawn breaks with its touch of pink
blushing, the city disappears in a grey haze, neon-tinged.

Seeing

Shut tight against the light
green corroded unhinged
ones hanging on to walls
that wore mildew moss &
lichen;

the whole city ghostly, an
apparition rising from the
dark moonlit sea, like some
old forgotten sepia tinted
photograph touched up

here & there with fluorescent
tints. Or a Russian castle
gone to ruins, its turrets
fallen, its towers ruined,
all the colour seeped out;

now a deserted pale shadow
of itself, wearing windows
that refused to see. Broken
battered their bars gone,
yet now they are owners of

unseeing eyes, now they
looked down on burning

pavements and would not
lift their eyes, now they
were prisoners of old ways

that refused to look at life.

Jewel eyes

Lit only by fireflies, the jewel-eyed night
stirred, its sights
pale opaque iridescent memories
teasing out shadows,
to escape
a searching fire,
when asked for more light!

The train-whistles at midnight remain
distant sounds that
teeter dangerously close,
eyes shut tight
against
onslaughts of imaginary
departures. A system of silent mores...

Records of an imperfect time, as always

in folders of lost memory
    those misty, white beginnings
  perfect wonder
illusory
    dreamlike transient stirrings;
            anticipation and waiting.

        If asked point-blank, maybe I'll say it's a
rainbow,
        all the accumulated hours and moments
      gathered together
    in the heart
  & how they paint
    a contradictory universe
        lit up with nothing but dreams. And fireflies...

Perception

Seeing You

It was a quiet evening
a little rain,
no, no metaphors
or tears
just rain, simple & plain, some tea.

The cup rattled a bit though
as a storm brewed in its leafs,
thunder clapped its hands in glee
and the curtains shook
in the wild breeze that rushed in.
and suddenly I saw... saw...

saw the elaborate charade, the cloak & dagger
notions - all tangled illusions! Waded in, trying to dismantle
outer reaches first, smug things that
hinder, separate, polarize, precipitate
distinctions

from an opal sky, its stars alien lands so far away from home.
Home? Trapped debris of a shelter long gone;
smashed it too....came out and saw you standing on the extinct
doorstep,
all thresholds bared, my mouth agape, Your formless form

studded with a billion stars!

Good to be alive
heart beating
thud thud boom boom
'You still there?
Are you there...?'

'No I am not.... it is your imagination speaking!'

Sound of laughter...
booms

I smile.
The tea is still surprisingly warm!

Gods, In Words

In the tender inner corners of the mind where God hides herself,
where over-explanation, intrigue, idiotic interpretations do not
disturb Her peace/His calm, there is an old almirah on which she
hoists Herself, right on top; it is a haven literally, of all those words
we don't usually find as everyday norm. There He sits for hours
looking at them, playing with them, throwing them down at passers-
by in mirth, who are left scratching their heads, of them, there's no
dirth! Here are a few that fell off the high perch: fugacious,
adumbrate coulrophobia, pogonophile, eucatastrophea, absquatulate,
luculent, sesquipedalion, amphisbaena, oh, there's more where they
came from! If you don't beat a

hasty retreat, they'll soon come out and meet, albeit dragging their
reluctant feet, being born in Greece. Some have roots in Sanskrit and
most are born in England of course. To our subcontinental vibes,
they hold a magnetic lure, we who do three languages or four with
ease, a linguistic tour embedded in our lips, so yes, here's some more
: blatherskite, duende, frondeura, funambulista, amphibologya,
eurhythmic, exequies, lollygag, lycanthropythe, exsanguine
anfractuous. Oh my God, how can one ever think of putting them all
up in symmetric streams of poetic verse, these unknown, disparate
words, so like the millions of us out there, calling different names to
God, then calling each other names because the names of our Gods
don't match! Then calling Him/Her to descend the high perch and
watch us at these absurd games! Perhaps we begin with a deep silence
in our hearts.... for the One & the Same.

To You

On the opposite bank of the sea of Humanity,
lives a demon with a raging river in its mouth,

One night it swelled & spilled & came tumbling
out on to the streets & lanes, every place on earth

awash with doubt, almost every town a
grisly story awaiting apocalypse, dreading the dirth

of kindness, or darkness that lives beyond the
dawn, oh! What a time to be born & breathing in

insalubrious climes that claim the end is well nigh
near! Bells ring out loud & clear as little babies

tumble and fall, their mothers' arms bereft, shorn
of care, waiting for waves to crash & snare their

hearts: still forever.

What a time, oh what a time it is, oh dear, whatever
happened to all that we held dear? Thin partitions

holding up all that separates, that terrifies, that take
away lives because of the image on prayer sites,

because of the contents of food & semi-circular
irrelevant authoritarian forms that allow us to die,

because some of us will never comply with unkindness
or with gloom. We shall go looking for brooms to sweep

up the debris, go looking for light to spark up the kindness
that is ours, the inner light that a hunt for material numerical

success shrouds into invisibility, and that we shall uncover
reveal, unfold, so a thousand demons are slayed, and

a thousand stories of our victories are told! Rise, O' One of Light
O *Mahishasurmardini*, One without fear, it's your time to be here!

Treasure

Stimulus

Node

Reptile like tentacles, flung
        out, branches snagging

foot slipped. Full stop.

Anti-node

tentacles hold, balance empowers
        and rest is history, or is it the

future? Proceed…

Check back later, progress tracked
via moon-beams, Twitter (@night)
bird-song, leaf-veins, water-beds

that had cried
and dried long ago,
now checking.....

again.

Looking for Treasure

Ground Zero

On a dry hot day
the sheep. The men. The land.

Not yet parched, signatures due
On parchment, so water can flow.

Ground water tables turned again
and again, and again, each year it

goes on. Until this. It is gone now
on a cool spring day.

Forgive & Treasure

Some dew had remained on the grass, leaves
on trees, glistening in its sheen, trembled at
the touch of faraway winds, pearls fell off like

tears in the earth. It was an act of forgiveness:
as the brown earth soaked it all up - all it received,
even the tiniest little twig or blessing, deep graves

dug into an aching bosom, no room for craving nor
trepidation, just fissures where everything meshed,
and erupted into myriad kaleidoscopic treasures!

It is the earth's way - transforming dust & compost
Into gems of yore, a deeply ingrained eternal allure,
abiding forever in its clay, it was there yesterday,

It's here today: a sense of forgiveness, a rule so pure!

Go I Know Not Where

In search of a dream
I enter the sacred forest
tonight...

It whispers softly to me
with darkening eyes of green,
deeply inviting
and recklessly tumbling over
boulders of time.

Walking into
ever-widening
moonlit, silver circles
that float in mid-air,
is an eerie feeling,
like walking into a moment
and looking down.

Have you ever tried it --
walking into a moment & staying there,
gripping hard, not letting go
as a mountaineer would
cling on to an icy surface?

Through the soft glow &
gentle sway of trees,

awnings loom up, slowly,
and flow into torrents
as swift as the streams
gleaming in the moonlight.

Shapes form, and disappear
and form again,
outlining geometries
that hold meaning.

Once-upon-a-time homes
light up like an old flame
or fireflies,
just fragments of a moment,
then all is a hushed, dark whisper once again.

Out of the deepening gloom
to the slow beat of pensive drums,
they both appear on a sea of rolling green,
two cities together, in their timeless allure;
all lights ablaze & bands playing
the 'ethnic' song :
'I shall go aboard',
momentary ships
passing in the night....
nothing less &
nothing more.

And now,
clouds, ice,
turquoise wine
flavoured tea & primrose,
sit at table
sharing home-made bread
with a friend back home
after voyages
golden, divine.

All the bullion
is to reach darkened homes,
so the heart stays right!

An unhurried pink
touches the sky
in slow, loving sweeps.

The forest stirs awake...
All fragrance &
Full bloom.

Broom-Song

An ancient old old song that lay buried underground
came gushing out one day like storm water when I
dug at the opening in the sunlit balcony clogged and
watertight with debris of unknown origin, I dug deep
with a found object - a broomstick thick brown sturdy.

'Tum jo mil gaye ho, toh ye lagta hai...ke jahan mil gaya....'
The mist-enraptured car tottering dangerously close to
worlds of romance, vanishing almost, becoming mist
becoming cemented enclosures of approved addresses
In the midst of glittering citadels erect over hovels...hutments.
..jhopris...

I sweep with a rare joy, the collected dust and debris
swept aside, showing up red squares of shining floor,
clean, free of clutter, awakened to new openings. The
sun comes in with warm hues, and spotting it, Piano,
the musical cat, saunters up, meows and settles there;

I proceed with the broom, loving the way the dust
responds to its touch and comes up on the pan
when nicely invited with a helping hand. There's nothing
quite like dusting a floor, ok maybe sweeping comes
close, with a long handled mop, but dusting is an old fav.

At the cafe, when I am early and the all-in-one guy starts

off with mopping, having put the coffee in the machine,
I look at his expert sweep and wonder if he'll miss the spot
at the foot of the table, but can never be too sure. Partly
because I'd have to stare hard, stare closely, and it'd be rude.

Looking at new ways of unobtrusive observation...
songs on the floor
songs on shells
songs in the heart
songs
songs all around…

Songs, more songs

(*Tum jo mil gaye ho, toh ye lagta hai…ke jahan mil gaya — Ever since I am with you, it feels like the whole world is mine)*

To Verse

There was a lit-up magic
in the spring evening, you
& I, everyone & everything
sprinkled with star-dust, we
spoke up for the right things!

Oh, how we wore our poems,
& danced in our verse to meet
up with the evening star.... a
distant galaxy came right up
close & personal and mingled
from so far!

Oh, how close we all were!
You and I, the moon & the sky,
stars, flowers, & almost everything.

An Equal Earth

Frozen seas inside of me
thawed with warmth from
glowing pages of wisdom,

Droplets of ice and imagination
sparkle jewel-like, out in the sun,
rose-madder thoughts afire with

hope:

of freedom, of beauty, of just
endings to beginnings carved
in roses, sandalwood, fire, earth

sacred notions bound to
each other in holy threads
flowing for lifetimes...

in oceans of tranquility
an equal earth.

Arcs of Love

Love, a gossamer dream floating on mountain tops, a misty cloud
unseen,
    hidden gems in warm hearts,
      precious gifts
          evergreen.

Like gold in the furnace, or a trek through trees, summer clouds, cool
evening breeze
    you softly whisper, you don't have to speak, reaching deep
within
        where the pain is, where the hurt soaks, broken bits of our
own hopes
          we had thought lost forever, gathered in your
warm embrace,
            O behold love, how you heal!

        Where there is no hurt, no pain, not yet; you make an arc
of a circle,
      a rainbow, a leaf in the rain, a steady glowing grace arching
across the

      hours, where we dance together.... in wind, storm, high-
water or rain...

          You
        make
      of turbulence

a touchstone
& turn
it into a
light
golden
winged
swan,
unnamed.

Lost junction

It's a bit like the centre of a
spider's web - filaments of
long tender moments coming
together, melting and leaving
into a void of unknown untested
strings...

It is a junction where the future
comes to find out what it needs
to bring! Masses of lights, spread-
eagled, spangled, criss-crossed
run into and through each other,
striking up conversations that may

never have happened any other place!
It's a junction where you may hear
haunting blues, smoky dreams, even
songs from a whole new being,
What you can do with an hour of
waiting, is something worth seeing,

A poem could be jolted into
being, an elephant saved. A forest
recovered from dead debris, a song
sung in honour of spring,
so many, so many things.

Will the lost junction
reach you to your
favourite scene...?

Seeing infinity...

Infinity :
a moment
of suddenly seeing a
fleeting truth
and sitting there
transformed!

Infinity is metamorphosis...

Infinity is also
years of patient endeavour
to arrive at that moment
of simple truth, a new beginning,

of infinite possibilities...

Infinity is in the tiny atoms
that join together to form
everyone & everything.
Infinity is you, me,
the salt & the sea

big oceans & tiny streams.

Infinity starts from
a small idea
and becomes the

entire universe, a magical thing.

Infinity is made of endless strings
separate & together,

the choices that are ours
in the blink of an eye,
the road that is right
when all others have
been tried,

and found wanting!

Infinity is just round the corner
after the dark abyss has
been blinded
by light.

Three Emblems

Three emblems I choose for myself
this beautiful turbulent spring of '16,
the tiger, the tree
and a heart
evergreen;

Three emblems I'd love to gift you
this beautiful turbulent spring of '16,
the tree, the tiger
and a heart
evergreen;

Three emblems I'd gift the world
this beautiful turbulent spring of '16,
the tree, the tiger
and a heart
evergreen...

Reality

Calm Before the Storm *(a ghazal)*

Look how the roses sway in summer breeze this beautiful morn,
their sleepy buds unaware, their world calm before a storm!

Azure, ivory, cerulean, wonder writ large on a waiting sky,
will it turn deep purple when the rain clouds hit a storm?

Will you wait with me to see how lightening streaks the sky,
or would you rather be by yourself in this calm before the storm?

Take this, take this blue talisman and keep it close to your heart,
whenever a storm breaks, know we are together, not miles apart!

The writing on the sky is clear: love the darkness just as you do light,
for it is in dark times the world is set right, storm or no storm!

What do you cherish my friend? So, go do as you please; but once
call me your name, O friend, in the clamour of thundering storms!

I see you far away, looking at your night sky, and I hold your hand,
call you my name, & there you are: smiling away, a calm before the
storm!

You Girl!

Impossible flights enmeshed in your hair,
                              your dreams
      they shatter faint illusions, chase dark shadows into streams
         where stalks of grass and pebbles wash them in rainbow hues,
               you put them in elegant rose-strewn vases, blue lights of
shanties, chandeliers or palaces,
                  soak them in resplendent beams;
                     flights of transcendence, your dreams!

Laughter & gaiety soar in you,
      plumes from the very heart of despair,
   where once there was a yesterday – hopeless and torn asunder,
                  there's now today, salvaged, oh wonder of wonders!
Your utter courage rests
                  warmly now, under a cat's snug basket of brown wicker!
Those lemon-chilli strings, are they still with you?
Or lying flat out at traffic junctions from where you went to school,
hand-in-hand with a good Samaritan?
Those deep dark wintry days in December in the country's warm
heartland so true.

Freedom (*Aug 15, 2017*)

70 in '17: there's so much heart-break under hoisted dreams...
Where are those open skies, those tumbling free-flowing streams,

Of human kindness? Why is the brown earth full of love unseen?
Her surface neon-lit, her gems scorched of precious gifts? Her

people rushing onwards into abysses of their own darkening
deeds! A red flare up there, though visible in its

 eloquent glare, an

angry fit it's left to smoulder by itself, alas, it is a morning of
reckoning.... the way ahead is stormy and full of turbulent

Meandering

        Wayward

R i   ck et y
Pathways

Falling steeply into

                    ravines...

You & I, I & you

All we can do

Is hold hands, holding up our dreams....

For you & me..& liberty...Aug 15, 2017

Reality
Four Layers

Its invisibility is a fabric that binds
The net around us, wrapping tight

Since birth, in layers of confining
roles, one upon the other, quite

determined to keep it watertight,
neat layers of hessian, coarse

mesh, muslin and fine silk, all
transparent yet invisible to the

onlooker from outside. Until one
tries to reach within and check

the inner textures - almost an
electric shock at the sameness

that exists! No wonder it is not a
prevalent practice. After all who

would want to shear the centuries
of their belief? The eyes look away,

the hands do not dare plunge into

depths that would unravel the pile

of carefully constructed shelves,
moving instead to corners where

there are no betraying quirks.

Will you?

Sing me a duet, please

One in which Meera drops her voice a half-notch,

Sita sacks the dhobi, a deep frown impaled on her brow

So smooth, so innocent;

While Draupadi yearns for

Years of instruction

At a haloed portal of learning,

Her sacred tryst with destiny!

Not tethered, nor bound like fists,

She yearns for years of learning…

So sing me a duet please…

(Meera, Sita, Draupadi - characters from Indian epics, mythology)

Song Sung Together

There's a floating song sung like a dream just within reach,
it is a fairytale palace in the middle of an ocean or just
a pebbled sandy beach,

and you are there, I see you, your book of verse in hand,
your fragrant floral garland that even the Gods envy, for
its erudite strands,

you connect hearts & minds, cultures and people of different
kinds, you restore me to myself, if ever I've been left
in despair, and restore

others too, when they find you, your words, your love, your
mercy, that embraces and upholds like a safety-weft
all around, oh you are right there

in the middle of it, spinning away silken threads of togetherness
for yourself and for others, thousands and thousands of strands
of belonging and mercy,

and beauty.

Noir

I
take a smudge of kohl and
   let it fly out into the wind;
      an imaginary, invisible trajectory
         no one can see.

          The heart believes,
        and deeply at that
      it protects, it disfigures
     to ward off
   evil eyes unfair!

I
Look up eyes closed,
   hands cupped in prayer
      just like beautiful devotees
         in loved spaces held dear:

a billowing open sky,
   a patient gentle tree,
      a warm friendly heart
        a happy memory....

I
touch them all with kohl
and keep them in my heart,
remembering smudged foreheads

in baby photographs.

Then I remember.

I
weep in silence,
lost tears
to dry parched
acres of loss.

Acres and acres of loss.   Acres and acres of loss.
I look up, eyes flowing, for forgiveness....we could not save her.

To you, O Tiller!

At the complex intersections

of
  'enough-bereft-
        -surplus-threadbare-
 flying-walking-
        -sore-safe'

      spaces that we inhabit,

our make-believe happy points (very real)

located on a tear-drop that refuses to dry,

balanced precarious, perched,

at the edge of

Us

&

Them :

An old old divide that only death can breach,

Or a sudden revelation - like the red-marching-wave

that swept the city off its feet,

without disturbing a single
time-line!

Kudos. congratulations. For connecting us back to something deep
within us, O, gentle, untiring folks! You have lighted up the hearts!

We who celebrate poetry and art and life, will not be doing so in vain.

Lost

A song rises, my heart its beating rhythm, rare freedom
out there; but misty-eyed I wonder, where the birds have gone!

They were here all along, on leaf & branch, even just this very morn;
when I look out now, I wonder where the birds have gone.

Aeons away, or right now in azure-awash skies, remembering
the soft touch of their flights, I wonder where the birds have gone.

Hope is a light turning into dawn, we shall wait for them to return
on branches of trees newborn; now I wonder where the birds have
gone.

In a lighted funnel of dust a melody rises, its mist full of dreams
of forests dark and green where birds abound, I know where the
birds have gone,

To wait out this winter of want, these lanes of trees & leaves shorn,
they have gone
into darkness, their soft sighs dying in the night, I know where the
birds have gone.

      To wait out this winter of want in the very heart of spring,

           to which we've been
                    blind so long

our blindness a sign of the

                      times;

           how long before

new blooms are born ?

Colour

In a lighted funnel of dust a melody rises,
to see where the birds have gone,
in this winter of want,
where the leafless lanes mirror our vices!
Are the birds now in darkness, soft voices
looking for a glow, shadows of a light lost
in cemented spaces where the trees had a home,
is that where the birds have gone, fleeing high-rises?
Skies wide open, in welcome, bring out the blues,
the whites, the cerulean & azure, multi-hued choices
all ours in a sea of green, lighting up spaces
that had lost their shine. Now they glimmer with hues
of fresh new shoots, a greening of minds that seize
the moment, look at new truths & are full of surprises!

Darkening Bright

The sky rolls wayward, wildly careeering, as if about to fall;
      it gathers its forces in an ominous call, is it
           Armageddon?
   In the city - dark,
        in the city - light,
            in the city -a darkening bright!

The sky rolls over, toppling sideways, it holds on to stars;
      it is omniscient, omnipresent, almighty
        but unable to break its fall!

  the world hurtles towards a darkening bright
     where thousands of people die: brutal nights,
         haven't you heard?
            world, world: a darkening bright!

The sky crashes around, on its way to the earth,
      an Armageddon in equal parts
        darkness & light,
      it'll be a close
        fight,

        hold
      on to your light,
    your light-sabres, your

crystal clear eyes, your light...

light..... light.... more light.....in a world that's darkening bright.

In an Ancient Land

In
The Land of Two Epics, Spring 2016
Article 377:
Illegal Deeds,

The Fatherland, Summer 1936
Articles X Y Z:
Illegal Beings!

The Land of Liberty, Autumn 1836,
Article A B C:
Illegal: Rights,

The Land for All- World, Rains, 20XX
Article 123:
Illegal: Injustice!

It will rain, it will rain,
Justice for all, one day,

Women, Trees
Rivers, Beings
All Orientations
& Dreams...

Shall we balance the equations
Once & for all...?

Do you believe in magic?

Yes I do. The good-times kind when life is a merry-go-round of pure happiness, but even more, the dark-times kind that happens in the darkest hours, a magic touch of love pulling you out of abysses too deep and too dark to fathom alone.

Filaments, glimpses, tendrils, striations, reverberations, lighted rays and luminescence of its presence you might have felt all around, but it took special effort on your part to put together its whole being almost like a jigsaw created out of awareness, knowledge, sincerity, kindness, curiosity, tender faith and a heart full of gratitude. When it rose up in the shape of a kind loving caring powerful being of infinite tenderness, you knew that in your heart of hearts you'd always been right - fairies and magic do exist!

Invincible Dust

Invincible dust is multicoloured
inclusions of soft rays of the
melting sun from everywhere,
in its tiny being are immense
stories of the world: ancient
Persia, Asia, Eurasia, Far East,
Egypt, Africa, Europe, America
& ancient civilisations that have
ceased to exist; leaving behind
tales entwined in a golden mist
flying all around, suffused with
warm picturesque unifying dust
that carries one and all in
its embracing arms!

Revered Dust

If Social Reformer Rebel Poet Namdeo Dhasal Could Speak to Dust

Dust, revered dust, in sunlit channels you abound,
dancing waif-like, happy, carefree, in all seasons
year-round ! When the rain comes you mingle in its
merry streams, losing yourself without a thought,
such assurance as yours, kings would envy and
unknowing, for years remain fraught!

Earlier I did fancy myself as dust, O dust!
But now I know how much depth you ensconce
in your tiny frail spare form! It is not about feeling
small, insignificant, unheard, unnerved or just
forlorn. Dust, you've been flying high on your own
ever since time began; and you have the power, the
knowledge, yours the immortal song, so how could
I ever think I was like your own? I have aeons to go
before I learn, to be without a form, an ego, a self so
unknown and of importance shorn, that it'll be centuries
before I lose myself like you, O, dust,

You have my deepest reverence forever & anon!

*Dhasal said he found happiness in poetry...... . In an interview in 1982 he said
that if the aim of social struggles was the removal of unhappiness, then poetry was*

125

necessary because it expressed that happiness vividly and powerfully. Later he stated, "Poetry is politics." Dhasal adhered to this principle in his private life. He told the photographer Henning Stegmüller, "I enjoy discovering myself. I am happy when I am writing a poem......"

Dharu-Hera and Dhasal (*for whom dust reigns*)

That golden hour of home-coming,
'godhuli logno' in rustic Dharu-hera,
a dust storm rises,
    akin to music
      of the silent spheres,
         and the silent mind :
            captivating,
                caressing the soul,
  becoming the dream,
    becoming time,
      becoming the dust

      of their hooves,

becoming the hide of their multi-coloured skin!

That golden hour of home-coming,
'godhuli logno', in ravaged Golpitha,

126

A slow stormy magic unravels
before the eyes, like a dream...

*To Dhasal who had discovered the voice of dust..... the thirsting, urging layer of
poetry & justice hidden in dust, in decay, in crumbling edifices and oppressed
people.... in exploited women and hungry children....beaten men...
He had come home at the golden hour, carrying their voices in poetry......*

'Golpitha' is one of his poetry collections, named after a ragged Mumbai location.

Dust in raptures

Dust in raptures

R
   o
       l
          l   s

            &

               T
                 u
                   m

                       b l
                         e
                                s
                          e
                    s
                i
              R

and   s h i n e s

Fusing into light,
It arrives on the other side,

Intoxicated,
Un s t e a dy

Unprimed!

There are continents submerged in its depths
Starry nights covering its sighs;
There's poetry in it
            and there is
                  every musical tide;

An entire earth pushes to emerge
From its invisible womb, into tiers of rolling light!

Dust in raptures

what a
sacred

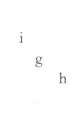
        s
          i
         g
           h
            t!

Delight d e l I g h t   del I g h t
de lIght   delIghtdel I g ht

Publisher's list

If you have enjoyed *Where I Belong, moments, mist and song,* **consider these other fine books from Mwanaka Media and Publishing:**

Cultural Hybridity and Fixity by Andrew Nyongesa
The Water Cycle by Andrew Nyongesa
Tintinnabulation of Literary Theory by Andrew Nyongesa
I Threw a Star in a Wine Glass by Fethi Sassi
South Africa and United Nations Peacekeeping Offensive Operations by Antonio Garcia
Africanization and Americanization Anthology Volume 1, Searching for Interracial, Interstitial, Intersectional and Interstates Meeting Spaces, Africa Vs North America by Tendai R Mwanaka
A Conversation…, A Contact by Tendai Rinos Mwanaka
A Dark Energy by Tendai Rinos Mwanaka
Africa, UK and Ireland: Writing Politics and Knowledge ProductionVol 1 by Tendai R Mwanaka
Best New African Poets 2017 Anthology by Tendai R Mwanaka and Daniel Da Purificacao
Keys in the River: New and Collected Stories by Tendai Rinos Mwanaka
Logbook Written by a Drifter by Tendai Rinos Mwanaka
Mad Bob Republic: Bloodlines, Bile and Crying Child by Tendai Rinos Mwanaka
How The Twins Grew Up/Makurire Akaita Mapatya by Milutin Djurickovic and Tendai Rinos Mwanaka
Writing Language, Culture and Development, Africa Vs Asia Vol 1 by Tendai R Mwanaka, Wanjohi wa Makokha and Upal Deb

Zimbolicious Poetry Vol 1 by Tendai R Mwanaka and Edward Dzonze
Zimbolicious: An Anthology of Zimbabwean Literature and Arts, Vol 3 by Tendai Mwanaka
Under The Steel Yoke by Jabulani Mzinyathi
A Case of Love and Hate by Chenjerai Mhondera
Epochs of Morning Light by Elena Botts
Fly in a Beehive by Thato Tshukudu
Bounding for Light by Richard Mbuthia
White Man Walking byJohn Eppel
A Cat and Mouse Affair by Bruno Shora
Sentiments by Jackson Matimba
Best New African Poets 2018 Anthology by Tendai R Mwanaka and Nsah Mala
Drawing Without Licence by Tendai R Mwanaka
Writing Grandmothers/Escribiendo sobre nuestras raíces:Africa Vs Latin America Vol 2 by Tendai R Mwanaka and Felix Rodriguez
The Scholarship Girl by Abigail George
Words That Matter by Gerry Sikazwe
The Gods Sleep Through It by Wonder Guchu
The Ungendered by Delia Watterson
The Big Noise and Other Noises by Christopher Kudyahakudadirwe
Tiny Human Protection Agency by Megan Landman

Soon to be released
Ghetto Symphony by Mandla Mavolwane
Of Bloom Smoke by Abigail George
Sky for a Foreign Bird by Fethi Sassi
Denga reshiri yokunze kwenyika by Fethi Sassi
A Portrait of Defiance by Tendai Rinos Mwanaka

131

Nationalism: (Mis)Understanding   *Donald Trump's Capitalism, Racism, Global Politics, International Trade and Media Wars, Africa Vs North America Vol 2* by Tendai R Mwanaka

Ashes by Ken Weene and Umar O. Abdul

Ouafa and the Thawra: About a Lover From Tunisia by Arturo Desimone

Thoughts Hunt The Loves/Pfungwa dzinovhima Vadiwa by Jeton Kelmendi

When Escape Becomes the only Lover by Tendai R Mwanaka

Litany of a Foreign Wife by Nnane Ntube

https://facebook.com/MwanakaMediaAndPublishing/

Printed in the United States
By Bookmasters